LEEK

HISTORY TOUR

First published 2020

Amberley Publishing
The Hill, Stroud,
Gloucestershire, GL5 4EP
www.amberley-books.com

Copyright © Neil Collingwood, 2020
Map contains Ordnance Survey data
© Crown copyright and database
right [2020]

The right of Neil Collingwood to be
identified as the Author of this work
has been asserted in accordance with
the Copyrights, Designs and Patents
Act 1988.

ISBN 978 1 4456 5771 4 (print)
ISBN 978 1 4456 5772 1 (ebook)

British Library Cataloguing in
Publication Data.
A catalogue record for this book is
available from the British Library.

Origination by Amberley Publishing.
Printed in Great Britain.

ACKNOWLEDGEMENTS

My thanks go to the late Geoffrey and Jean Fisher, Sue Fox, Richard Furmston, Mr Philip and Mrs Muriel E. Shepherd, the staff of Leek Public Library and the Staffordshire Fire & Rescue Service. My sincere apologies if I have omitted anyone from this short list of contributors.

ABOUT THE AUTHOR

Neil was born in Junction Road, Leek, in 1956 but moved away to Newcastle-under-Lyme when he was aged just two and a half. He says that Leek always felt like home and he continued to visit the town regularly to see his grandparents, who all remained there. Neil was glad to move back to Leek twelve years ago and intends to stay in the town.

Neil's interest in local history started when he obtained a six-month contract working at Newcastle-under-Lyme Borough Museum. While there he became interested in their historic photographs and ended up cataloguing the museum's entire collection. He stayed on as a volunteer archivist one day per week for a further seven or eight years and during that time co-compiled two books featuring Newcastle photographs.

Neil has now had fourteen books published: thirteen on local history, along with the first ever *Atlas of Dragonflies and Damselflies of Staffordshire*, compiled for the City of Stoke-on-Trent Museum. He now works full time carrying out local history research, which he uses in his books and in the regular articles he contributes to the weekly *Leek Post & Times* newspaper.

INTRODUCTION

Leek is a small north Staffordshire market town located close to the borders with Cheshire and Derbyshire. The town is described as being 'on a hill in a valley', an appropriate description as Leek sits on a 'plug' of Sherwood sandstone left by the wearing action of the River Churnet, which loops around it. Beyond the town the land rises significantly: in the north to the heights of the Roaches (from the French *roches* – 'rocks'), in the north-east to a long ridge called Morridge, and in the south-west to Ladderedge, scaled by the road to Stoke-on-Trent and beyond.

Leek appeared in the Domesday Book of 1086, which stated 'Rex ten Lek' – 'the king holds Leek'. For centuries the town was almost exclusively concerned with pastoral farming and the marketing of its produce, but then in the seventeenth to nineteenth centuries Leek became a major centre for the silk industry, both for dyeing and the production of threads, fabrics and garments. The mill owners gained great wealth but were also great benefactors to the town: the Nicholson family funded the Nicholson Institute and the war memorial, the Hall family funded Methodist chapels and schools, and the Wardles supported many important charities.

The silk industry was still strong in the early twentieth century but then began to suffer from foreign competition and by the 1960s and 1970s the mills were contracting and closing rapidly, unable to compete with countries like China and India. Today the town still boasts many large mills, but these either stand empty and forlorn or have been converted to other purposes. Leek still boasts a thriving weekly livestock market and its streets are filled with small independent shops. It is, as Leek people say, 'a place out of the noise'.

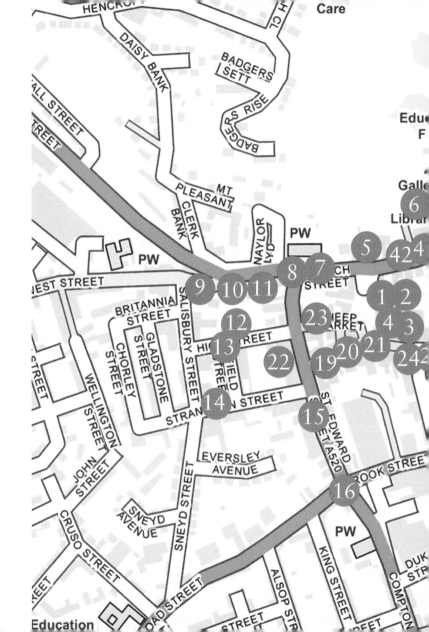

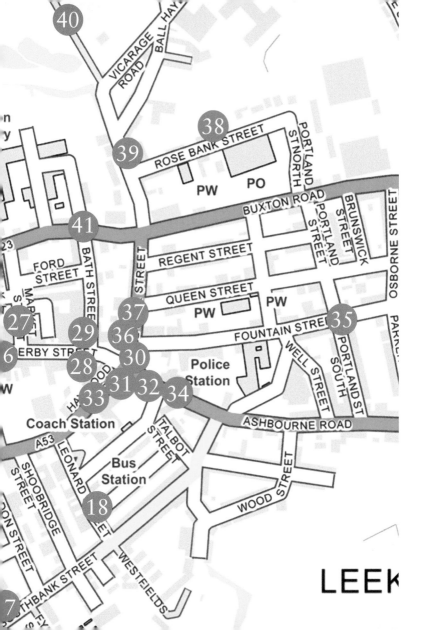

KEY

1. MARKET PLACE

Despite its small size Leek has always boasted a large number of public houses – fifty-two within living memory, but more than 150 over time. Perhaps unusually, Leek had two pairs of pubs next door to one another. This photograph shows the Cock Inn (now The Beer Dock) and the Red Lion in Market Place. The Red Lion began life as a two-storey, half-timbered private house and has just reopened after a few months of closure.

2. THE RED LION

Like many pubs the Red Lion began its life as a private house. It is believed to have been built around 1607 for Thomas Joliffe, a wool merchant, but by the early nineteenth century it had been converted into a coaching inn. This photo shows an empty shop between the Red Lion and the entrance to its yard and stables. This shop and archway stood on the site of the Butter Market – designed by J. T. Brealey and built in 1897.

3. MARKET PLACE

This photo shows the horse-drawn equivalent of a Rolls-Royce dropping off its passenger at the Red Lion in Market Place. Both passenger and 'driver' are immaculately turned out and the passenger's moustache has plaited ends that extend 6 inches downwards below his chin. In the background is Robert West's watch and clock shop (demolished *c.* 1930), complete with the clock provided for public convenience. This clock's duty is now performed by the one on the Butter Market.

4. THE BIRD IN HAND

The Bird in Hand was transformed in 1889 from the humble timber-framed building shown here into the towering three-storey mock-Tudor building it is today. Its seven barley-twist stone chimneys with castellated tops are impressive and would now cost a small fortune to have carved. Some years ago the large wooden boss hanging beneath the gable on the Sheepmarket side of the pub crashed to the ground, and was sadly never replaced.

5. THE WHITE HART

The seventeenth-century White Hart Tearooms have been open next to the Foxlowe in Stockwell Street for at least 100 years, although not always so called. Previously they were Haworth's Tea Rooms – also licensed to sell tobacco. The premises were renamed the White Hart, although the Haworth name remained above the door for some time. Until recently there was a rather old-fashioned yet pleasant seating area upstairs, but this has now been replaced by self-catering accommodation.

6. THE NICHOLSON INSTITUTE

This photo shows the Nicholson Institute from the tower of the parish church of St Edward the Confessor – the 'old church'. In the foreground is the large bowling green that used to be located in the grounds of the Foxlowe. The buildings beyond the green are the buildings of Cruso's Yard, which were demolished and replaced by Moorlands House (1983), the offices of Staffordshire Moorlands District Council.

7. CHURCH STREET

This view shows the huge changes that have taken place in the area since the 1960s. The buildings in Church Street, including the Golden Lion, the Conservative Club and the George Hotel, were all demolished in 1972. Church Street was significantly widened and its junction with St Edward Street improved. In this photo the former Cock Inn, on the corner of the Market Place, has been demolished and is being replaced by new shops.

8. THE GEORGE HOTEL

The George Hotel stood opposite today's Green Dragon at the corner of St Edward Street and Church Street. By the 1970s both Church Street and this junction were impractical for modern vehicles and on one occasion a long commercial vehicle became stuck, paralysing through traffic. In 1972 the buildings on the east side of Church Street were demolished, as were later several at the top of St Edward Street, allowing both the road and the junction to be improved.

9. MILL STREET

This late 1950s view looks down Mill Street from Overton Bank. To the left are the public conveniences by William Beacham and West Street Club – formerly the police station. Housing on both sides is built against the steep sandstone cliffs, with many houses having no rear yards. Extensions or cupboards were created by simply digging into the rock. Towering over Mill Street was 'Big Mill', which was designed by William Sugden in *c.* 1857. How different this scene is today.

10. MILL STREET

This photo shows the view down Mill Street during demolition. Perched high above is the Maud Institute (1896), which has a notice in front stating 'Dangerous Building Operations No Heavy Loaded Vehicles Allowed'. In the sandstone cliff one of many cavities carved into the rock that allowed the houses to extend backwards from their otherwise small plots can be seen; this one appears to have been filled up with bricks from the demolition, saving on disposal costs.

11. CLERK BANK AND ST EDWARD'S CHURCH

This superb photograph shows Clerk Bank and behind it St Edward's Church, parts of which date from the fourteenth century. The scene is little different today except that the building in the left foreground, once the Beehive Inn, has been demolished. The three low buildings on Clerk Bank are cruck-framed and among the oldest in Leek. This vantage point is popular with visitors and has often been used on postcards.

12. THE GRAND CINEMA

The original Grand Theatre and Hippodrome was built by Samuel Salt after Field House was sold in 1908 and the grounds were released for development. After alterations it became purely a cinema in 1915, and further alterations bestowed the fashionable art deco appearance it retained until its closure in the mid-1980s. The block of flats that has replaced it was given the name Paramount House, a reference to Paramount Pictures, which was founded in 1912 and is still in business today.

13. FIELD HOUSE

Field House, or The Field, is a late Georgian house built for S&W Phillips (silk manufacturers) and later occupied by the Whittle family (also silk makers). In around 1907 the grounds were built over when the Globe Inn was demolished to allow the creation of High Street and Field Street. This photo shows the house prior to those alterations. For many years the house served as the Leek National Reserve Club, known locally as 'The Nash'.

14. STRANGMAN STREET

This photo, looking towards St Edward Street, shows Central Garage closed and awaiting new occupants. It later became French Finds, selling French antiques, but is now empty. Beyond the garage is what used to be a small Pentecostal church and then a stone building once occupied by Samuel Sigley's undertakers. The large building beyond is Whittle's cornmill. Whittle's did not limit themselves to selling flour, oatmeal, etc., but also cement and fertilizers and were even agents for Ind-Coope beers.

15. ST EDWARD STREET

This post-1897 view down St Edward Street towards Compton shows two horse-drawn traps and a scavenger's handcart. 'Scavenger' has various meanings, but here refers to a person employed to remove rubbish and 'hoss-muck' from the roads, something he appears to be doing with an implement similar to the snow scoops sold in supermarkets today. When you look at the amount of horse manure on some old photographs, it is easy to see how essential this service was.

16. THE QUIET WOMAN AND THE UNICORN

This photograph shows another example of two adjacent public houses. The present Arts and Crafts Unicorn building dates from 1897, and it seems likely that the group of workmen in this photograph are just about to commence demolishing its archaic predecessor. Sadly the Unicorn has now closed permanently as a pub and the next door Quiet Woman, formerly the White Hart, has opened and closed fitfully for the past few years.

17. ALL SAINTS CHURCH

Scottish architect (Richard) Norman Shaw designed All Saints Church, built in 1885–87. Some consider it to be the finest church he designed, and is the only Grade I listed building in Leek. To Shaw, architecture was an art rather than a science, and many of the details of All Saints reflect his support of the new Arts and Crafts movement. Today many visitors enjoy the stained-glass windows, wall paintings and embroideries as much as the building itself.

18. LEONARD STREET

When horses were the main means of transport a variety of tradespeople were required to care for them. In Leonard Street, Robert Hill's veterinary surgery operated from inside an archway surmounted by a stone-carved horse's head. The head still survives, although the vets is long gone. Hill must have done well, as by the age of fifty he had retired. The old Sugden police station, in Scottish Baronial style, can be seen lower down the street.

19. THE BAZAAR

The Economy Shopping Centre offered 'Quality and Reliability' and rather resembled a modern-day Wilko's. The windows and pavement outside were crammed with goods: baskets, garden tools, tennis racquets and buckets, to name but a few. Things are not always what they seem though, as behind the solid-looking art deco frontage the shop had a corrugated-iron roof and was therefore more like a barn than a shop. The author shopped here for toys as a child.

20. STANLEY STREET

Leek was clearly thriving in around 1915. Ladies walk briskly down the road carefully avoiding horse manure and a man sneaks a surreptitious glance at one he has perhaps taken a fancy to. On the corner of Derby Street is Thomas Riches' clothiers, now café Appolonia, and opposite the Queen's Head (Valiant) is Trafford's printer and newsagent. Outside Traffords's is a structure for securing a canopy to in sunny weather – something that would undoubtedly be forbidden today.

21. HARRIET HARROD'S SHOP

How much is that doggy on the step? It doesn't quite have the same ring as the well-known song, but Harriet Harrod's shop did stand on the corner of Dog Lane and Stanley Street, with access to the shop via a set of steep stone steps. The shop sold baskets, glassware and china. Although the cellar still exists, there is no sign of it now from the outside. The site is currently occupied by Elizabeth Marie homewares.

22. ST EDWARD STREET

This photograph shows the sequence of changes that took place after Field House (see No. 13) was sold off and High Street and Field Street were built over its grounds around 1908. Apparently Fallon's fruiterers and The Globe public house were not demolished simultaneously because here Fallon's still exists, The Globe has gone and Pickford's grocer's has already been built. Perhaps Fallon's obtained a stay of execution while they found new premises.

23. HIGH STREET

This long view of High Street from Sheepmarket shows two buildings that are no longer standing: Pepper's Garage and the Grand cinema. Here the Grand has a high triangular pediment rather than either the rounded gable it was built with or the art deco frontage with two columns that it had at the end of its life. The site of Pepper's Garage is currently a car park after standing vacant for many years.

24. JOHN WEST'S SHOP

In 1881 John West was a twenty-year-old ironmonger's assistant at Wooliscroft's shop on the corner of Russell Street and Derby Street. A decade later West had done very well for himself, having bought the shop, married and fathered two children. Also living with his family were his cousin, two boarders and two servants. The shop was ostensibly an ironmongers, but also sold sporting goods, including air guns, ceramic fire surrounds, oil, paint and even portable milking machines!

25. DERBY STREET

A view of Derby Street looking towards the Nicholson War Memorial around 1940. This view down Derby Street shows the half-timbered Roebuck and next-door Tatton's bakery and café, a Georgian building that was clad in 'fake' half-timbering to make it better match the Roebuck. The timber frames of half-timbered buildings were cut to size and put together in a joiner's yard with marks cut in the beams to show how they fitted together. They were then taken down again and transported to the site where they were re-erected.

26. THE ROEBUCK

The 1626 Roebuck is the only half-timbered Leek building that looks much as it did when built; most others having been refaced with brick. Some obvious changes are that the curved beams on the gables have been painted over plaster that covered the original beams and windows. The original large timber windows were replaced by the current small metal ones prior to 1873. Folklore states that the building was transported from Shropshire but there is absolutely no evidence for this.

27. THE 'NEW' TOWN HALL

The Town Hall in Market Street was built in 1878 as a private club and concert hall called Union Buildings. When it failed three years later it was bought and converted into Leek's second Town Hall. A large number of Leekensians feel that it should not have been demolished in 1988 as there is no longer anywhere to stage the sort of entertainments that used to take place there. The site is now a car park.

28. DERBY STREET

This photograph shows some of the many changes that have taken place in Leek. Sparrow Park was still the site of the livestock market and the Nicholson War Memorial ('The Monument') was not yet required. In the foreground was the Weights and Measures Office with its public weighbridge, and in the background Fountain Street Primitive Methodist Chapel and various Brough Nicholson & Hall mills – all now demolished. On the left are the Elizabethan-style public baths, which were demolished in 1975.

29. GETLIFFE'S YARD

At the end of the nineteenth century Leek's Improvement Commissioners stated that Getliffe's Yard consisted of nothing but brothels and dosshouses – officially 'common lodging houses'. Later three cottages were knocked together by Fred Hill for his printing business – presumably the three in the photo that have been repointed and bear the sign 'Getliffe's Design and Print'. Today the yard has been transformed into an attractive and stylish shopping arcade with a fully glazed roof.

30. DERBY STREET

This photo shows Sparrow Park at the bottom of Derby Street with its domed public conveniences. Over time the roads that Leek Town Lands Trust allowed to cross the park became so busy that a traffic island was created there. This floral roundabout successfully managed traffic without a major incident for eighty years until 2012 when Staffordshire County Council decided to remove it, despite a petition, an occupation and fierce and ongoing public protests against it.

31. THE TALBOT

The stone-built building seen here probably began life as the Rodney's Head, later becoming the Spread Eagle and then the Talbot. On the sign is a white hunting dog (Talbot), which gave the pub its name. The inn shown here was largely taken down in 1877/78 and rebuilt as the present Sugden building. This probably 1870s image shows a wedding party outside. In 2013/14 the Talbot was extended massively into a sixty-three-bedroom Premier Inn.

32. THE LEEK BATTERY LEAVING FOR FRANCE

The Leek Battery is passing William Sugden's Sanders Building, which was occupied at the time by J. Mears. Crowds line the route waving patriotically, but few could have anticipated the horrors that awaited their menfolk on arrival in France. Lieutenant Arthur Falkner Nicholson (pictured) would be wounded in the shoulder, and that incident would be partly responsible for his brother, Basil Lee Nicholson, being fatally shot through the head by a German sniper near Ypres in 1915.

33. THE OLD CATTLE MARKET

Leek's livestock market used to be located in front of the Cattle Market Inn and where the Nicholson War Memorial now stands. In the 1920s it moved across Ashbourne Road to where the Smithfield Centre is now. That was built in 1960 when the cattle market moved again to its present site in Junction Road. In this photograph, clearly taken on a Wednesday (market day), a Berresford's Hanley via Cheddleton double-decker bus stands ready to depart.

34. THE NICHOLSON WAR MEMORIAL

This photo is unusual in that only for a short time was it possible to see both the Nicholson War Memorial and the tower of the Nicholson Institute at the same time from the bottom of Ashbourne Road. This was made possible by the 1975 demolition of the former Leek public baths prior to the building of the much less attractive Britannia Building Society building. Leek's popular floral roundabout has also been lost.

35. THE ROMAN CATHOLIC CHAPEL

Leek's first Roman Catholic chapel opened in 1828 on the corner of Fountain Street and Portland Street. It was closed in 1864, when the first St Mary's Church opened in King Street. The old chapel briefly became a silk shade before being demolished and built over. The date stone from the old chapel, bearing the inscription 'D.O.M Deo Optimo Maximo MDCCCXXVIII' ('to God, best and greatest, 1828') is located in an outbuilding of the former Loreto Convent.

36. THE BETHESDA CHAPEL

Built in 1862 for the New Connexion Methodists, this chapel on the corner of Queen Street and Ball Haye Street later became the Bethesda Chapel. Having closed once in the twentieth century, it reopened for use by a different Methodist faction before closing permanently in 1963. It then became the base of operations for Riley's Recycling, where paper and cardboard were collected for pulping. Demolished in the late 1980s, the site is now a car park.

37. NO. 1 QUEEN STREET

At the time this photograph was taken Robert Wright, sewing silk manufacturer, would have been living in this fine house on the corner of Queen Street and Ball Haye Street. In the 1911 census he was sharing the eleven-room house with his son and daughter plus two live-in servants. Today the house is the premises of SBW Electrical. At the rear of the shop are some of Leek's few surviving courthouses, which are no longer occupied.

38. ROSE BANK HOUSE

Rose Bank House put a new slant on 'moving house' when the Co-op planned a new supermarket for Buxton Road. Disused factory buildings on the site were demolished to leave only Rose Bank House, a substantial Victorian villa, standing. The Sugden-designed house was 'floated' on a concrete raft, which was then ratcheted along concrete rails before coming to rest well out of the way of the store. This photo shows the house being emptied prior to the move.

39. ST LUKE'S VICARAGE

St Luke's Vicarage stands on a parcel of land purchased from the Ball Haye estate in 1856, the foundation stone being laid on the occasion of Revd William Dampier's wedding to Sarah Sleigh that year. The building was used by the church until the 1970s when a smaller replacement was built in Novi Lane. St Luke's House now houses the Moorland Veterinary Practice, and is obscured from this viewpoint by a screen of trees.

40. BALL HAYE HALL

In 1853 this house belonged to J&J Brough and was later rented to members of the Worthington family and then to John Hall – all silk manufacturers. Consequently, many Leekensians incorrectly refer to it as either John Hall's or Brough Hall. In the 1930s there was a plan to turn the hall into a hospital, but after the war the government redirected the money raised. It was later converted to council flats but was allowed to deteriorate and was demolished in 1972.

41. RAYNER'S SHOP

This property was occupied around 1908 by Rayner's and Sutton's, who would now be said to be involved in 'transport logistics'. At the time of this photo sisters Annie and Catherine Rayner were 'Rail Parcel Agents' and Suttons were general contractors and carriers, delivering via horse-drawn vehicles to 'All parts of the world'. Today this and the rest of New Street are unoccupied and possibly await future demolition by Buxton & Leek College.

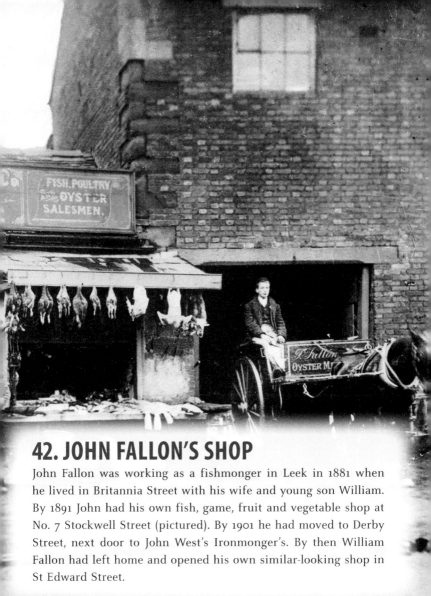

42. JOHN FALLON'S SHOP

John Fallon was working as a fishmonger in Leek in 1881 when he lived in Britannia Street with his wife and young son William. By 1891 John had his own fish, game, fruit and vegetable shop at No. 7 Stockwell Street (pictured). By 1901 he had moved to Derby Street, next door to John West's Ironmonger's. By then William Fallon had left home and opened his own similar-looking shop in St Edward Street.

43. LEEK FIRE BRIGADE

This photograph shows Leek Fire Brigade outside the fire station in Stockwell Street. This station, originally part of the stabling of the Cock Inn, was demolished and a new fire station built to the design of John Thomas Brealey in 1896. That station later became the Engine Room bar and is now Society. The brigade shown here included five members of the Carding family, it being traditional for sons to follow their fathers into the brigade.

ALSO BY THE AUTHOR